JUL   2009

Facts About Countries
Australia

Dana Meachen Rau

SEA-TO-SEA
Mankato Collingwood London

This edition first published in 2009 by
Sea-to-Sea Publications
Distributed by Black Rabbit Books
P.O. Box 3263
Mankato, Minnesota 56002

Printed in China

Library of Congress Cataloging-in-Publication Data:

Rau, Dana Meachen, 1971-
  Australia / Dana Meachen Rau.
    p. cm. -- (Facts about countries)
  Summary: "Describes the geography, history, industries, education, government, and cultures of Australia. Includes maps, charts, and graphs"--Provided by publisher.
  Includes index.
  ISBN 978-1-59771-112-8
  1. Australia--Juvenile literature. I. Title.
  DU96.R365 2009
  994--dc22
                                        2008004630

9 8 7 6 5 4 3 2

Published by arrangement with the Watts Publishing Group Ltd, London.

Facts About Countries is produced for Franklin Watts by Bender Richardson White, PO Box 266, Uxbridge, UK.

Editor: Lionel Bender
Designer and Page Make-up: Ben White
Picture Researcher: Cathy Stastny
Cover Make-up: Mike Pilley, Radius
Production: Kim Richardson

Graphics and Maps: Stefan Chabluk
Educational Advisor: Prue Goodwin, Institute of Education, The University of Reading
Consultant: Dr. Terry Jennings, a former geography teacher and university lecturer. He is now a full-time writer of children's geography and science books.

Picture Credits

Pages: 1: Corbis Images Inc. 3: Corbis Images Inc. 4: Hutchison Photo Library/Nick Haslam. 5-6: Corbis Images Inc. 7: Corbis Images Inc. 8: Corbis Images Inc. 9: Corbis Images Inc./Paul A. Souders. 10:Corbis Images Inc./ Richard Glover. 10-11 bottom: Corbis Images Inc. 12: Corbis Images Inc. 13: Corbis Images Inc.15: Corbis Images Inc. 16: Corbis Images Inc. 17: Corbis Images Inc. 18: Corbis Images Inc./ Howard Davies. 19: David Simson. 20: Corbis Images Inc. 21: Corbis Images Inc. 22-23 bottom: Corbis Images Inc./ Robert Garvey. 23:Veronica Strang. Lampeter University. 24: Corbis Images Inc. 25: Hutchison Photo Library/ R. Ian Lloyd. 26-27: Eye Ubiquitous/ Adina Tovy Amsel. 29: Corbis Images Inc. 30: Corbis Images Inc. 31: Corbis Images Inc. Cover photo: Corbis Images Inc.

The Author

Dana Meachen Rau is a full-time writer and editor of non-fiction books. She has written more than 10 books for children about countries of the world.

Note to parents and teachers

Every effort has been made by the Publishers to ensure that the websites in this book are suitable for children, that they are of the highest educational value, and that they contain no inappropriate or offensive material. However, because of the nature of the Internet, it is impossible to guarantee that the contents of these sites will not be altered. We strongly advise that Internet access is supervised by a responsible adult.

Contents

Welcome to Australia

Australia is the largest island in the world. It lies between the Indian and South Pacific Oceans in an area of the world called Oceania.

A land of contrast

Australia lies below the equator in the southern hemisphere. This means that its winter is from June to August, and summer from December to February. Australia has large, modern, busy cities along its coast. Its countryside, called "the Outback," is mostly empty, flat, and quiet.

Offshore Islands

Australia governs many islands around its coast. These include Christmas Island, the Cocos (Keeling) Islands, and the Coral Sea Islands. The largest of Australia's offshore islands is Tasmania. This was named after Dutch navigator Abel Tasman, the first European to visit the island. He landed there in 1642.

Below. **The center of the city of Melbourne is filled with modern skyscrapers.**

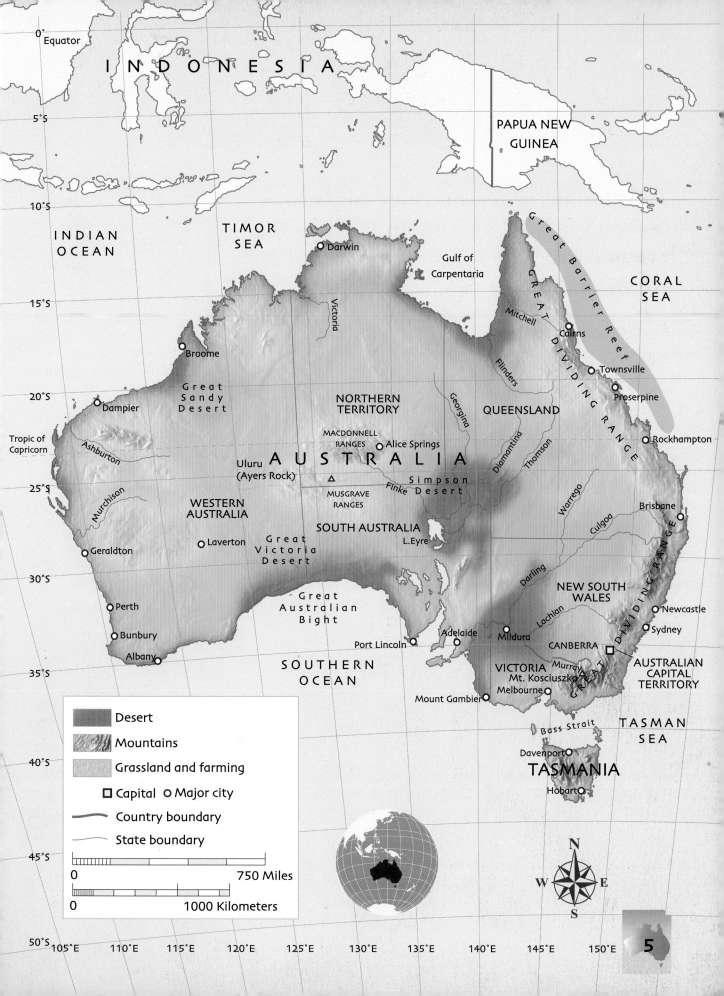

The Land

The climate in the north of Australia is wet and hot. In the center, it is mostly hot and dry. The rest of the country is warm and damp.

Grassland and land for livestock

Most of the high ground lies in the east, in the Great Dividing Range. Here, the land is covered in grassland and forest. In the center of Australia, only tough grasses and shrubs grow. This land is good for raising sheep and cattle but not for growing crops.

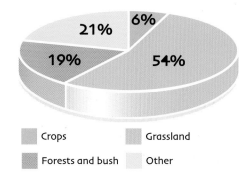

6%
21%
19%
54%

Crops Grassland
Forests and bush Other

Above. **How land is used.**

Below. **This forest of palms, eucalyptus trees, and tree ferns is in the southeast.**

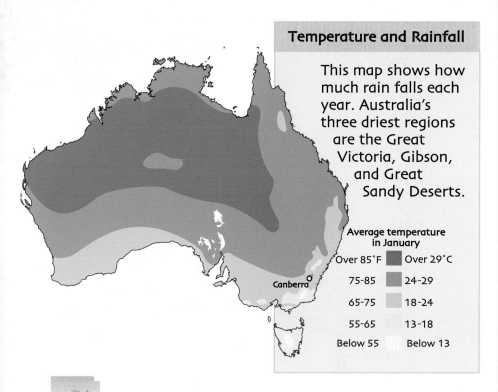

Temperature and Rainfall

This map shows how much rain falls each year. Australia's three driest regions are the Great Victoria, Gibson, and Great Sandy Deserts.

Canberra

Average temperature in January

Over 85°F	Over 29°C
75-85	24-29
65-75	18-24
55-65	13-18
Below 55	Below 13

Deserts and forests

The west of Australia is mostly a raised, flat region of very dry deserts. In the center is Uluru (Ayers Rock), the world's largest single block of rock, 1,100ft (330m) high.

Most rain falls along the coast, where more people live and work than elsewhere in Australia. Rainforests grow in the north and south of the country.

Right. **A red kangaroo.**

Below. **Comparing the summer and winter temperatures in five different cities.**

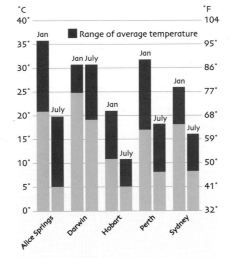

Web Search ►►

► **www.gbrmpa.gov.au**
About the Great Barrier Reef.

► **www.bom.gov.au**
Australian weather and climate.

► **www.ga.gov.au**
For maps of Australia.

The People

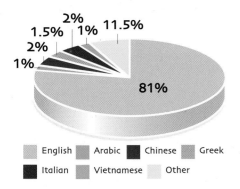

2%
1.5% 1% 11.5%
2%
1%
81%

English | Arabic | Chinese | Greek
Italian | Vietnamese | Other

Above. **Most people in Australia speak English, but there are also many native languages.**

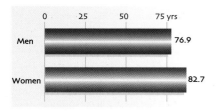

	0	25	50	75 yrs
Men				76.9
Women				82.7

Above. **Age men and women can expect to live to.**

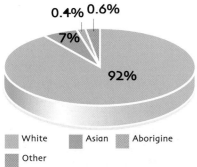

0.4% 0.6%
7%
92%

White | Asian | Aborigine
Other

Above. **Different races in Australia.**

Right. **An Aboriginal hunter. He is holding traditional weapons, including a spear and a boomerang.**

Australians are mostly a mix of native people, the Aborigines, and people whose families came from Europe and Asia in the 1800s and early 1900s.

Ancient ways of life

The Aborigines came to Australia about 40,000 years ago from Asia. They hunted with spears and boomerangs and gathered food from the land. People around the world have learned about Aboriginal history and beliefs from their cave and rock paintings, which are found all over Australia.

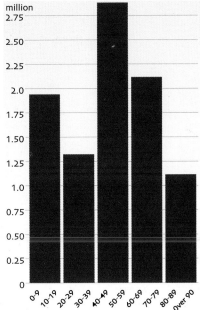

Above. **Numbers of people of different ages in the Australian population.**

Left. **The parents of these children playing at an outdoor party came to Australia from many different countries.**

People from all over the world

British settlers were the first newcomers to Australia, in 1788. They came to farm or raise sheep. In the 1850s, many people from China arrived to work in gold mines.

Since 1945, more than five million people have moved to Australia from more than 150 countries. Today, there are fewer than 800,000 Aborigines. Most live in the cities and towns, but a few still live in the Outback in the same way as their ancestors did.

Web Search ▶▶

▶ **www.immi.gov.au**
Details about immigrants to Australia.

▶ **www.aiatsis.gov.au**
About Aborigines and other Australians.

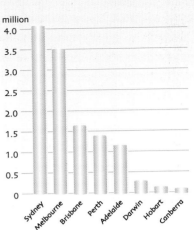

million
4.0
3.5
3.0
2.5
2.0
1.5
1.0
0.5
0

Sydney Melbourne Brisbane Perth Adelaide Darwin Hobart Canberra

Above. The number of people living in Australia's main cities.

Below. A long, straight road in central Australia. Many roads in the Outback look like this.

Above. This house in the suburbs of Brisbane is built of bricks and wood, with a tiled roof. It is like the houses built by the first British settlers in Australia in the early 1800s

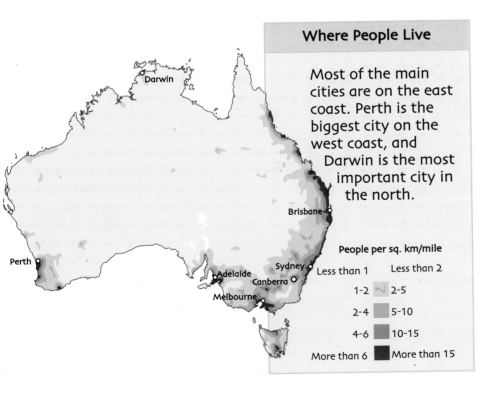

Where People Live

Most of the main cities are on the east coast. Perth is the biggest city on the west coast, and Darwin is the most important city in the north.

People per sq. km/mile

Less than 1	Less than 2
1-2	2-5
2-4	5-10
4-6	10-15
More than 6	More than 15

Town and Country Life

More than 85 percent of Australians live and work in cities in the south-eastern corner of the country.

Big cities

The capital city of Australia is Canberra, but Sydney has more people. Sydney is the main commercial city and has the biggest port. Melbourne, the second-largest city, is another huge business center.

Web Search ▶▶

▶ www.cityofsydney.nsw.
gov.au
Sydney's official website.

▶ www.act.gov.au/index.jsp
Canberra's official website.

▶ www.flyingdoctor.net
The Royal Flying Doctor
Service.

Life in suburbs and countryside

Most people live in single-story family houses in the suburbs that surround the cities. These houses have gardens and verandas where people can relax in the evening after work.

Life in the countryside is very different. People there are mostly farmers, fruit-growers, or miners. Many farms are so large that people need to drive to see their neighbors. They may visit the nearest town for supplies only once a week. Their houses are big, with space for the family to live and work. There are barns for storage.

Farming and Fishing

Two-thirds of Australia is used for farming or grazing. Fishing is carried out along the coast.

Raising animals, growing crops

Most land is used as grazing for cattle and sheep. There are 150 million sheep in Australia. Their wool is the main export. In many parts of the country, it is difficult to grow crops because of flooding and droughts.

Australia produces butter, cheese, and yogurt. Many farmers keep poultry and 90,000 chickens are sold for meat each year. The main crops are sugarcane, wheat, and barley. Farmers also grow rice, oats, cotton, and vegetables such as carrots, potatoes, and tomatoes. Australian fruits include oranges, pineapples, grapes, and apples.

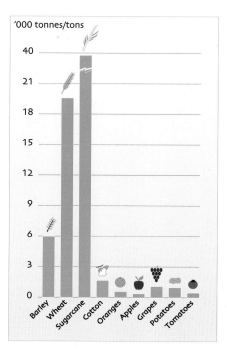

'000 tonnes/tons

Above. **Quantities of the main crops grown each year.**

Right. **Wheat is harvested from a farm in Western Australia.**

12

The fishing industry

Offshore fishing boats catch mostly marlin, tuna, shrimp, lobsters, and oysters. Many of the shellfish are sold to Japan. Oysters, shrimp, and even crocodiles are raised in fish farms and artificial lakes.

Left. Sheep are sheared once a year. The merino sheep is the most popular type. It produces beautifully soft, fine wool.

Right. Weights of fish and shellfish caught by sea-going boats.

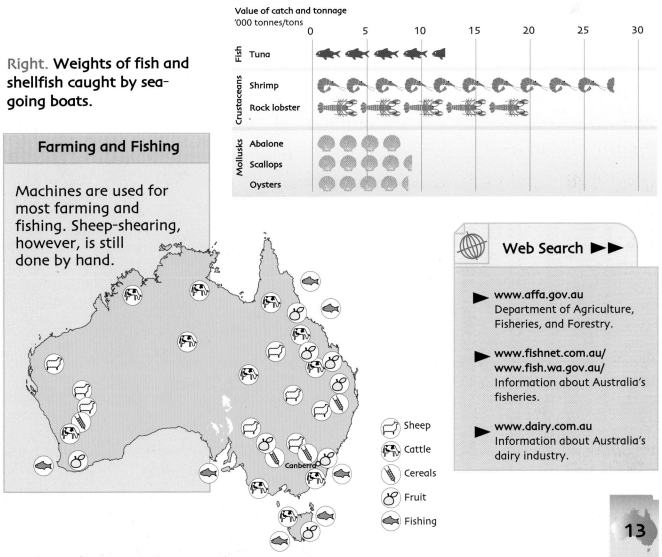

Value of catch and tonnage
'000 tonnes/tons

		0	5	10	15	20	25	30
Fish	Tuna							
Crustaceans	Shrimp							
	Rock lobster							
Mollusks	Abalone							
	Scallops							
	Oysters							

Farming and Fishing

Machines are used for most farming and fishing. Sheep-shearing, however, is still done by hand.

Canberra

Sheep
Cattle
Cereals
Fruit
Fishing

Web Search ▶▶

▶ www.affa.gov.au
Department of Agriculture, Fisheries, and Forestry.

▶ www.fishnet.com.au/
www.fish.wa.gov.au/
Information about Australia's fisheries.

▶ www.dairy.com.au
Information about Australia's dairy industry.

13

Resources and Industry

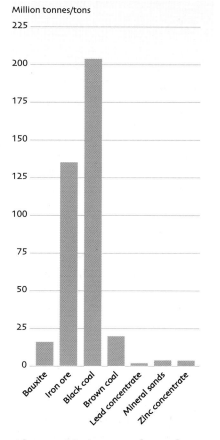

Above. **Main metals and other minerals produced.**

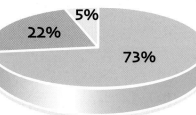

Service industries   Manufacturing industry

Agricultural industry

Above. **Types of work. The service industry has the most workers.**

Australia is rich in natural resources, especially minerals. These are mined and treated to make many goods. But few people work in mines or factories.

Metals, fuels, and precious stones

The main minerals are iron, bauxite, coal, lead, and zinc. Other metals mined include silver, copper, nickel, tin, uranium, and gold. Oil and gas are produced in large amounts. Valuable stones such as opals, diamonds, rubies, and sapphires are also dug from the ground.

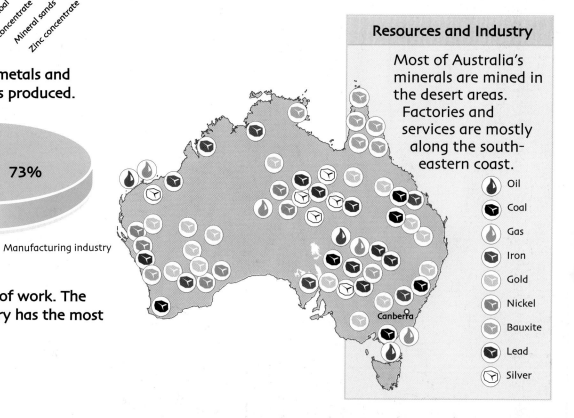

Resources and Industry

Most of Australia's minerals are mined in the desert areas. Factories and services are mostly along the south-eastern coast.

- Oil
- Coal
- Gas
- Iron
- Gold
- Nickel
- Bauxite
- Lead
- Silver

Canberra

Major industries

Australia is one of the world's largest producers of meat, dairy products, and animal feed. Other industries include chemicals, plastics, electronics, paper, and steel. Factories make machinery, vehicles, and home appliances such as ovens.

Most of Australia's workers are in the service industry. They include teachers and people working in banks, post offices, shops, restaurants, hotels, and government offices.

Right. **At this mine in Western Australia, huge machines scrape iron ore from the rocks.**

Transportation

In Australia, distances between places can be so great that a good system of transportation essential. Road travel is the most popular, but railroads and airlines are used a lot, too.

Roads and railroads

There are nearly 620,000 miles (1,000,000km) of roads, connecting all of the major cities. Cars and buses carry people. Large trucks, called road trains, pull heavy cargoes across the Outback. There are more than 11 million registered motor vehicles in Australia.

The Trans-Australian Railway takes goods from factories and mines to seaports. Australia's trains also carry some 600 million passengers a year. The Indian-Pacific Railway, a luxury train, takes tourists across the whole country, from Sydney to Perth. There are no trains in Tasmania.

Below. **Road trains pull many trailers behind them across the vast Outback.**

Boats and planes

Australia's main ports include Sydney, Melbourne, and Brisbane. They handle passenger and cargo ships. There are more than 400 airports, but most handle only internal flights. Sydney Airport is the busiest international airport.

Above. This Boeing 747 belongs to Qantas, Australia's international airline.

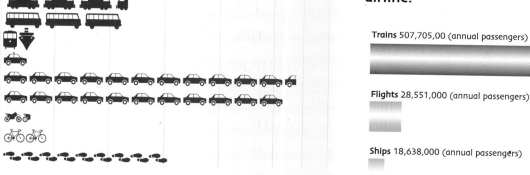

Above. The different ways Australians travel to work.

Trains 507,705,00 (annual passengers)

Flights 28,551,000 (annual passengers)

Ships 18,638,000 (annual passengers)

Above. Numbers of passengers carried on Australia's railroads, roads, and waterways.

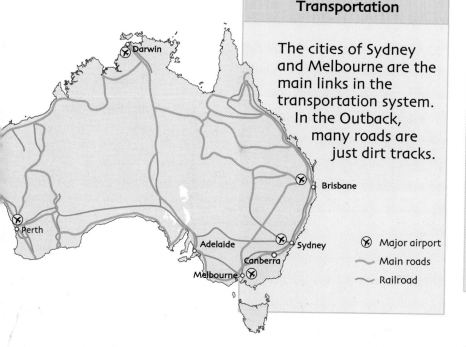

Transportation

The cities of Sydney and Melbourne are the main links in the transportation system. In the Outback, many roads are just dirt tracks.

⊗ Major airport

〜 Main roads

〜 Railroad

Web Search ►►

► www.atcouncil.gov.au
The Australian Transport Council.

► www.rta.nsw.gov.au
About roads and traffic in New South Wales.

Education

For Australians, the school year starts in January or early February and ends in December. In the Outback, where there are no towns, Schools of the Air provides a way for children to learn.

School age and the school day

Children go to school from age six to age 15 or 16. Primary and secondary education are free, but some children go to private, fee-paying schools. Classes start at 9 A.M. and end around 3:30 P.M. After school, children go home to study or go to sports practice.

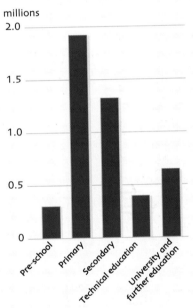

Schools of the Air

The Schools of the Air program was set up in 1950. Students tune in to a two-way radio to talk with a teacher far away. The service has now been improved with new telephone and Internet technology.

Above. **The number of pupils being taught.**

Left. **These university students in Melbourne are studying the geography of Australia.**

School and beyond

Children start primary school at the age of six. After Year 6 or 7, they enter secondary school, where they stay until Year 10. Children study science, Australian history, mathematics, English, music, and art. When they are 15 or 16, students can leave school and go to work, or go to a college that will train them for a job. After this they can go on to study at a university.

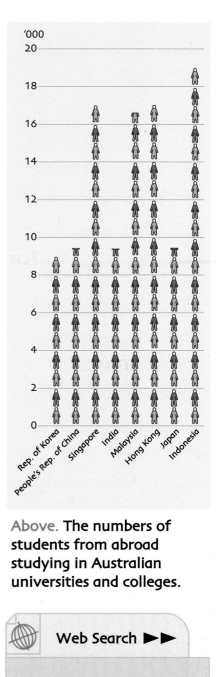

Above. **The numbers of students from abroad studying in Australian universities and colleges.**

Above. **A group of children from a primary school take a break on an outing to a museum.**

Web Search ▶▶

▶ www.dest.gov.au/
Commonwealth Department of Education, Training and Youth Affairs.

▶ www.dete.sa.gov.au/
Departments of Education for Western and South Australia.

Sports and Leisure

The warm climate allows Australians to take part in a wide variety of outdoor sports. More than one-third of the population plays organized sports.

Sports and pastimes

Children play many games including netball, cricket, tennis, soccer, rugby league, rugby union, Australian Rules football, and hockey. On the coast, surfing, swimming, scuba-diving, surfboat racing, sailing, and fishing are popular. Elsewhere, pastimes include hiking, cycling, horseriding, tennis, badminton, polo, and golf. Netball is the most popular sport among women.

Australian Rules Football

"Aussie Rules" is a rough and active game. It was first played in 1858. In September each year, more than 100,000 people gather to watch the Aussie Rules Grand Final game held in Melbourne.

Right. **Sailing in Whitsunday Passage, near the Great Barrier Reef.**

Above. **Australian Rules football is a mix of soccer and rugby. It is a fast and furious game.**

Right. **Membership of different sports clubs.**

Sporting Heroes

Australia's world-class sportspeople include Rod Laver, Margaret Court, Pat Cash, and Leighton Hewitt in tennis; Donald Bradman, Rodney Marsh, and Shane Warne in cricket; Jack Brabham in motor racing; Catherine Freeman in athletics; Ian Thorpe in swimming.

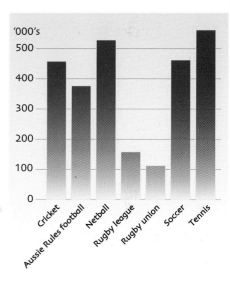

Olympic spirit

In 2000, Sydney hosted the 27th Summer Olympic Games. Stadium Australia was built in the city to hold the athletics events. Australians were proud to be chosen to host the Olympics in such a special year, and to be recognized for their sporting tradition.

Web Search ►►

► www.australia.com/
Australian Tourist Board site.

► www.acb.com.au/
Australian Cricket Board site.

► www.afl.com.au/
Australian Rules football site.

Daily Life and Religion

In Australia, a family normally wakes up at around 7 A.M. The working day is usually from 9 A.M. to 5 P.M.

Healthy living outdoors

Children spend their free time playing sports or going to the Boy Scouts or Girl Guides. With their parents, they may go to the beach or visit a national park or shopping mall. In fine weather, Australians often have a "barbie" (barbecue) outdoors.

Australia has its own army, navy, and air force, which people can join when they reach the age of 17. There is a public healthcare system, paid for by the taxes that all workers pay. Children and the elderly get free healthcare.

The Royal Flying Doctor Service

In the Outback, the doctor's office may be hundreds of miles away. In an emergency, the Royal Flying Doctor Service (RFDS) sends medical staff out in small planes. Patients are treated on the spot or flown to the nearest hospital.

Below. **Families relaxing on the beach in Perth.**

Below. **Numbers of cars, telephones, and TVs for every 1,000 people in the population.**

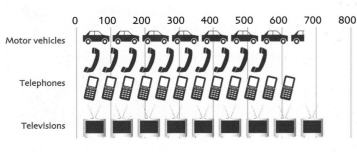

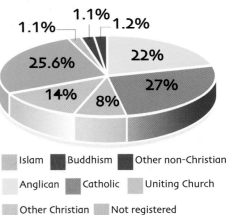

1.1%	1.1% 1.2%

22%

27%

25.6%

14%

8%

Islam   Buddhism   Other non-Christian

Anglican   Catholic   Uniting Church

Other Christian   Not registered

Above. The percentage of Australians following each main religion.

Web Search ►►

► www.aihw.gov.au
About health and welfare in Australia.

► www.catholic.org.au
The Catholic Church in Australia.

► www.defence.gov.au
The Department of Defense.

Above. Aboriginal rock art about Dreamtime—their story of Creation.

Religion

Most people in Australia are Christians, but Islam, Buddhism, and Judaism are also practiced. Aborigines keep up their traditional beliefs of "Dreamtime" and the spirit world.

23

Arts and Media

The mix of peoples in Australia has brought an amazing choice of magazines, radio stations, and television channels.

Music, dance, and art

The government helps pay for many arts events. All main cities have art museums, orchestras, opera companies, and theaters. The Aboriginal people have a lively artistic culture. At corroborees, they gather to dance and play music. Aboriginal paintings depict people, animals, and mythical creatures on bark, cave walls, or wood.

Australia's Most Popular Song

The most popular traditional song of Australia is called "Waltzing Matilda." It was written in 1895.

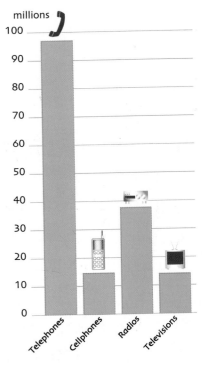

Above. **Total number of electronic goods.**

Left. **The Sydney Opera House, completed in 1973, is a famous landmark.**

Above. **Shoppers are entertained by dancers at an arcade in Cairns, Queensland.**

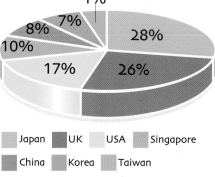

4%
7%
8%
10%
17%
28%
26%

Japan | UK | USA | Singapore
China | Korea | Taiwan

Above. **Where Australia's tourists come from.**

The media, broadcasting, and tourism

More than 1,200 magazines and newspapers are published in Australia. The *Australian* is the country's only national daily newspaper.

The government runs the Australian Broadcasting Corporation (ABC), which provides radio and television without commercials. There is also a number of commercial radio and television stations.

More than four million people visit Australia each year. They relax on beaches, visit historical sites, trek through rainforests, and admire the Great Barrier Reef.

Web Search ▶▶

▶ www.abc.net.au
The Australian Broadcasting Corporation.

▶ www.smh.com.au
The Sydney *Morning Herald* newspaper.

▶ www.ozco.gov.au
The Australian Council for the Arts.

▶ www.cultureandrecreation.gov.au/
A website with links to dance, movie, theater, and museum sites.

Government

Australia is a democracy based on the British system of government. Australia was once a British colony but became an independent nation in 1901.

Voting system

The head of state is Queen Elizabeth II. She does not rule Australia, but appoints a governor-general to represent her. Members of parliament are elected by people aged 18 or over. In Australia, people who can vote must do so and are fined if they do not.

Below. **The Australian parliament meets in this building in Canberra.**

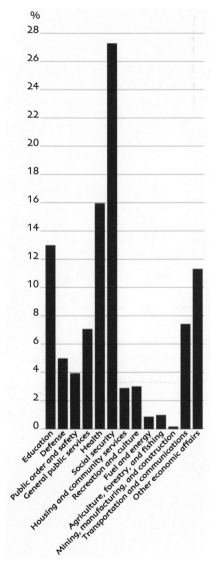

Above. **What the government spends on different services and industries.**

States and Territories

This map shows the six states and two territories that make up Australia.

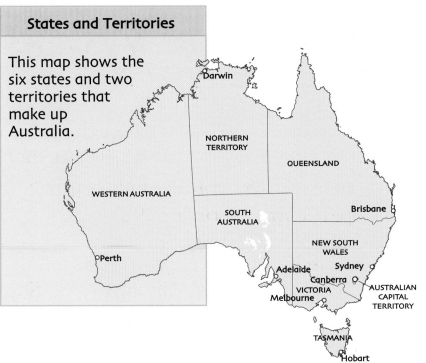

- Darwin
- NORTHERN TERRITORY
- QUEENSLAND
- WESTERN AUSTRALIA
- SOUTH AUSTRALIA
- Brisbane
- Perth
- NEW SOUTH WALES
- Adelaide
- Sydney
- Canberra
- VICTORIA
- AUSTRALIAN CAPITAL TERRITORY
- Melbourne
- TASMANIA
- Hobart

Who Governs What?

The government is in charge of defense, income taxes, and immigration policy.

The state and territorial governments oversee the police, education, healthcare, and transportation. Local councils are in charge of housing, roads, and waste disposal.

The prime minister

The House of Representatives makes the laws, which are then voted on by the Senate. Members of the House and Senate belong to political parties. The leader of the biggest party becomes the prime minister. He or she chooses members of parliament to make up the Cabinet, which helps the prime minister make decisions. States and territories have their own governments.

DATABASE

How parliament is organized

The House of Representatives has 148 seats. Representatives are elected for up to three years. The Senate has 76 seats. Senators sit for six years. Each state and territory elects its own members of parliament.

Web Search ►►

► www.australia.gov.au/
The Australian government's website.

► www.aph.gov.au
The Australian parliament's website.

► www.pm.gov.au
The Australian prime minister's official website.

27

Place in the World

DATABASE

Important dates

40,000 B.C.E. Aboriginal peoples arrive

C.E. 1600s Dutch explorers visit

1770 Captain James Cook claims eastern Australia for Great Britain

1788 British colony for criminals set up at Botany Bay

1851 Gold rush begins

1901 Independence from Britain

1927 Canberra becomes capital of Australia

1967 Aboriginal peoples win the right to vote

2000 Sydney Olympics

Australia plays a major part in the politics and economics of Southeast Asia because of its size and location.

Exports and imports

Australia earns a lot of money from its exports, most of which go to Japan. Among the main exports are farm products (including wheat and wool), minerals and other raw materials, and manufactured goods. Coal and cotton are exported, too. Tourism brings in a lot of money. Australia's main imports are cars and computers, and these come from the European Union (EU), the United States, and Japan.

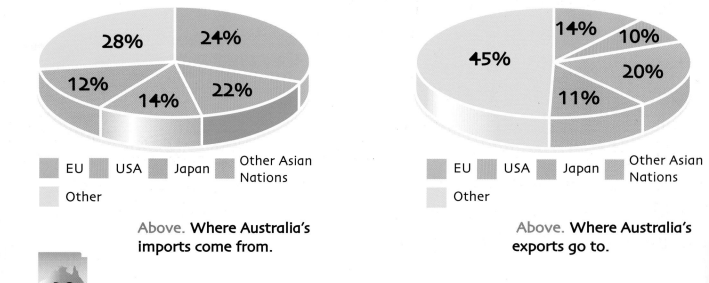

EU   USA   Japan   Other Asian Nations

Other

Above. **Where Australia's imports come from.**

EU   USA   Japan   Other Asian Nations

Other

Above. **Where Australia's exports go to.**

Above. **The Great Barrier Reef is more than 1,360 miles (2,200km) long and is home to more than 10,000 different species.**

Below. **Major exports, in billions of Australian dollars.**

Billion A$

Looking to the future

The arrival of people from different countries in the last century has helped the Aborigines. They have finally been given the right to claim back land that was taken from them in the past by white settlers.

Today, Australians are thinking about breaking their links with Britain. In a vote held in 1999 more than half voted against doing this, but the debate continues.

Area: 2,966,152 sq miles (7,682,300 sq km)

Population size: 19,169,083

Capital city: Canberra (population 298,000)

Other major cities: Sydney, Melbourne, Brisbane, Perth, Adelaide, Darwin, and Hobart

Longest river: Murray-Darling River system (2,094 miles/3,370km)

Highest mountain: Mount Kosciuszko (7,313ft/2,229m)

Flag:
The Australian flag has a background of dark blue, with the Union Jack of the United Kingdom in the upper lefthand corner. Under it is a star called the Commonwealth Star, which represents Australia. The other half of the flag shows the constellation of the Southern Cross, with five stars. The stars are white.

Official language: English

Currency: Australian dollar (A$)

Major resources: Coal, iron, bauxite, lead, zinc, oil, gas, silver, copper, nickel, tin, tungsten, gold, uranium, and manganese

Major exports: Aluminum, beef, coal, iron ore, bauxite, wheat, wool, machinery, and vehicles

National holidays and major events:
New Year's Day (January 1)
Australia Day (January 26)
Regatta Day, Tasmania (February)
Commonwealth Day (March)
Good Friday, Easter Saturday, Easter Day, and Easter Monday (March or April)
ANZAC Day (April 25)
May Day (first Monday in May)
Mothers' Day (May)
Queen's Official Birthday (June)
Fathers' Day (September)
Melbourne Cup Day (November)
Christmas Day (December 25)
Boxing Day (December 26)
Proclamation Day (December 26)

Religions:
Christian (Roman Catholic, Anglican, Uniting Church of Australia, and others), Islam, Buddhism, Judaism, Hinduism, Sikhism, Baha'i, Aboriginal traditional beliefs, Chinese traditional beliefs

Key Words

ABORIGINAL
Related to the Aborigines, the native peoples of Australia.

BAUXITE
Rock containing aluminum.

CLIMATE
The average weather conditions experienced in one area over a period of time.

COLONY
An area of land that is taken over, settled, and ruled by another country.

ECONOMICS
The study of business, money, industry, and resources.

EQUATOR
An imaginary line around the middle of the globe. It divides the northern and southern hemispheres.

EXPORTS
The goods and services a country sells to other countries.

DEMOCRACY
A system of government in which people freely vote for representatives for a fixed length of time.

DROUGHT
Long periods without rain.

GOVERNMENT
The organization that sets and enforces laws for a nation.

GRAZING
Feeding on grass and shrubs in fields and open areas.

IMMIGRATION
When people come from one country to live in another.

IMPORTS
The goods and services a country buys from other countries.

LIVESTOCK
Animals that are raised on a farm for their meat, milk, wool, and skins.

MANUFACTURED
Products made from raw materials using machinery.

POPULATION
The number of people who live in a certain area.

RESOURCES
A country's supplies of energy, natural materials, and minerals.

SERVICE INDUSTRIES
Industries that provide a service to people rather than make products.

SUBURBS
Areas of housing surrounding city and town centers.

Index